D1325376

LIFE'S LITTLE
TREASURE BOOK

On
Friendship

H. JACKSON BROWN, JR.

RUTLEDGE HILL PRESS

NASHVILLE, TENNESSEE

Published in Nashville, Tennessee, by Rutledge Hill
Press, Inc., 211 Seventh Avenue North, Nashville,
Tennessee 37219.

Distributed in Canada by H. B. Fenn and Co., Ltd., 34
Nixon Road, Bolton, Ontario L7E 1W2. Distributed in
Australia by Millennium Books, 33 Maddox Street,
Alexandria NSW 2015. Distributed in New Zealand by
Tandem Press, 2 Rugby Road, Birkenhead, Auckland
10. Distributed in the United Kingdom by Verulam
Publishing, Ltd., 152a Park Street Lane, Park Street, St.
Albans, Hertfordshire AL2 2AU.

Typography by D&T/Bailey Typesetting, Inc.,
Nashville, Tennessee

Illustrations by Ken Morris
Jacket illustration by Greg King

Book design by Harriette Bateman

ISBN: 1-55853-420-2

Printed in Mexico by R. R. Donnelley & Sons

2 3 4 5 6 7 8 9—04 03 02 01 00 99 98 97

INTRODUCTION

*W*hat is more welcome than the sound of a friend's voice, the sight of her smiling face, the warmth of an embrace? It is one of life's finest blessings to have a friend with whom we can safely discuss our fears and enthusiastically share our dreams— someone who accepts us totally as we are in spite of our shortcomings.

A true friend encourages us, comforts us, supports us like a big easy chair, offering us a safe refuge from the world. A true friend stands at our side during the best and the worst of times. A true friend listens when we need to talk through a problem. A true friend answers the phone at midnight and does not resent the call. A true friend will defend us to the world.

We speak of "friends and acquaintances" because we know the difference. Acquaintances we meet, enjoy, and can easily leave behind; but friendship grows deep roots. Even when we are separated by time and distance, friendship continues to grow and mature. We've all had the experience of meeting an old friend after many years and discovering that we are able to renew our relationship as if the separation had only been a few minutes.

A Nigerian proverb advises, "Hold a true friend with both hands." True and faithful friends are indeed a treasure, touching our hearts and strengthening our spirit with their words, their touch, and sometimes by just their silent presence.

$\mathcal{B}$ecome the
world's most
thoughtful friend.

Offer to pay for parking and tolls when you are the passenger in a friend's car.

∽

Friendships are fragile things and require as much care in handling as any other fragile thing and precious thing.

—Randolph S. Bourne

*Friendship improves
happiness and abates misery
by doubling our joy and
dividing our grief.*

—Joseph Addison

❧

If you know a friend has
had a bad day, take her out for
coffee or maybe dinner.

$\mathcal{I}$'ve learned that . . .

. . . an act of love, no matter how great or small, is always appreciated.   —Age 22

. . . the importance of fame, fortune, and all other things pales in comparison to the importance of positive personal relationships.   —Age 50

$\mathcal{B}$e the first to say, "Hello."

∾

$\mathcal{B}$e forgiving of yourself and others.

∾

$\mathcal{T}$reat everyone you meet like you want to be treated.

Except in cases of necessity, which are rare, leave your friend to learn unpleasant things from his enemies; they are ready enough to tell him.

—Oliver Wendell Holmes

$\mathcal{D}$on't forget a person's
greatest emotional need is to
feel appreciated.

*Instead of loving your
enemies, treat your friends a
little better.*

—Edgar Watson Howe

*K*eep secrets.

∾

*C*ompliment three people
every day.

∾

*R*emember other people's
birthdays.

Blessed are they who have the gift of making friends for it is one of God's best gifts. It involves many things, but above all the power of going out of one's self and appreciating whatever is noble and loving in another.

—Thomas Hughes

$\mathcal{I}$'ve learned that ...

. . . the friend you just met can be a truer friend than the one you've known all your life.
—Age 23

. . . it's best to ask for what you need from your friends and not assume that *somehow* they'll just know.
—Age 34

My friends are my estate.

—Emily Dickinson

$\mathcal{R}$eturn borrowed vehicles
with the gas tank full.

∾

$\mathcal{T}$hink twice before
burdening a friend with a
secret.

∾

$\mathcal{N}$ever tell friends that they
look tired or depressed.

$\mathcal{I}$'ve learned that . . .

. . . my best friends are usually the ones who get me in trouble. —Age 11

. . . a good relationship between me and my family, my friends, and my business associates can be boiled down to one word: *respect*. —Age 56

One friend in a lifetime is much; two are many; three are hardly possible.

—Henry Brooks Adams

∽

To find a friend one must close one eye. To keep him . . . two.

—Norman Douglas

Cut out complimentary newspaper articles about your friends and mail the articles to them with notes of congratulations.

❧

Friendship is Love without his wings!

—Lord Byron

$\mathcal{I}$'ve learned that . . .

. . . a good friend is better than a therapist. —Age 19

. . . when you and your best friend move away from each other to attend different colleges, you start saying "love ya" at the end of your phone conversations. —Age 18

I've learned that . . .

. . . moving away from my closest friends was much, much harder to do than I ever thought it would be.   —Age 26

. . . there is a great thrill in making pickles and jellies with the same friend I used to make mud pies with.   —Age 60

If a man does not make new acquaintance as he advances through life, he will soon find himself left alone. A man, Sir, should keep his friendship in constant repair.

—Samuel Johnson

Surprise a new neighbor
with one of your favorite
homemade dishes—and
include the recipe.

∾

*A father's a treasure; a
brother's a comfort; a friend
is both.*

—Benjamin Franklin

Years and years of happiness only make us realize how lucky we are to have friends that have shared and made that happiness a reality.

—Robert E. Frederick

$\mathscr{I}$ve learned that . . .

. . . when I surprise an old friend with a phone call, it will seem like just yesterday that we last spoke. —Age 38

. . . no matter how much a friend promises not to tell anyone else, she always does.

—Age 16

*O*ld friends are
the best friends.

It is great to have friends when one is young, but indeed it is still more so when you are getting old. When we are young, friends are, like everything else, a matter of course. In the old days we know what it means to have them.

—Edvard Grieg

$\mathcal{I}$'ve learned that . . .

. . . sisters can be like best friends and best friends can be like sisters. —Age 34

. . . nothing beats a hot summer night, a car full of friends, the windows down, music playing, and whistling at boys! —Age 18

Be more prompt to go to a friend in adversity than in prosperity.

—Chilo

Each friend represents a world in us, a world possibly not born until they arrive, and it is only by this meeting that a new world is born.

—Anaïs Nin

$\mathcal{I}$'ve learned that . . .

. . . meeting interesting
people depends less on where
you go than on who you are.

—Age 51

. . . a smile, a "How are
you?" and a warm, close,
caring hug always give love,
faith, and hope.
—Age 54

*M*ake allowances for your friends' imperfections as readily as you do for your own.

❧

*G*ive me a few friends who will love me for what I am, or am not, and keep ever burning before my wandering steps the kindly light of hope.

—Anonymous

A true friend is the greatest of all blessings, and that which we take the least care of all to acquire.

—François de La Rochefoucauld

∾

To the query, "What is a friend?" his reply was, "A single soul dwelling in two bodies."

—Aristotle

*All men have their frailties;
and whoever looks for a friend
without imperfections will
never find what he seeks. We
love ourselves notwithstanding
our faults, and we ought to
love our friends in like
manner.*

—Cyrus

*T*urn enemies into friends by doing something nice for them.

❧

*A*sk for double prints when you have film processed. Send the extras to your friends in the photos.

$\mathscr{I}$'ve learned that . . .

. . . when I wave to people in the country, they stop what they are doing and wave back.

—Age 24

. . . you never realize how many wonderful friends you have until your car breaks down.

—Age 22

I've often wished that I had clear,

For life, six hundred pounds a year,

A handsome house to lodge a friend,

A river at my garden's end,

A terrace walk, and half a rood

Of land, set out to plant a wood.

—Jonathan Swift

A friend is someone you can call at 3 A.M. and say, "I'm in a jail in Mexico." And he says, "Don't worry, I'll be right there."

Hold a true friend with both hands.

—Nigerian proverb

$\mathcal{I}$'ve learned that ...

. . . you can never have too many friends. —Age 16

. . . warmth, kindness, and friendship are the most yearned for commodities in the world. The person who can provide them will never be lonely. —Age 79

The most I can do for my friend is simply to be his friend. I have no wealth to bestow on him. If he knows that I am happy in loving him, he will want no other reward. Is not friendship divine in this?

—Henry David Thoreau

Introduce yourself to your neighbors as soon as you move into a new neighborhood.

∽

When a friend becomes ill, remember that hope and positive thinking are strong medicines.

$\mathcal{I}$'ve learned that . . .

. . . the greatest test of friendship is to take a vacation together and still like each other when you return.

—Age 59

. . . my best friend and I can do anything or nothing and have the best time.   —Age 18

*Never injure a friend,
even in jest.*

—Cicero

❧

A friend is someone who knows you and loves you for what you were and who you are, and who also shares your hopes and dreams for who you can become.

The better part of one's life consists of his friendships.

—Abraham Lincoln

$\mathcal{I}$'ve learned that . . .

. . . I would rather have a best friend than a boyfriend, except maybe on Friday night. —Age 20

. . . a good friend is the one who tells you how you really look in your jeans. —Age 25

I awoke this morning with devout thanksgiving for my friends, the old and the new.

—Ralph Waldo Emerson

Love is only chatter, Friends are all that matter.

—Gelett Burgess

Surprise an old friend with a phone call.

❧

Don't take good friends, good health, or a good marriage for granted.

❧

Don't let a little dispute injure a great friendship.

$\mathcal{I}$'ve learned that . . .

. . . I need to let my friends comfort me and hold me up, to let them know I need support, that I'm not always as strong as I look or act.

—Age 49

. . . having a young friend when you are old is a special joy.

—Age 83

*From quiet houses and first
beginning,
Out to the undiscovered ends,
There's nothing worth the
wear of winning,
But laughter and the love of
friends.*

—Hilaire Belloc

$\mathscr{I}$'ve learned that . . .

. . . true friendship
continues to grow, even over
the longest distance. —Age 19

. . . in this world, you don't
need a multitude of friends.
All you really need is one
who will stand by you
through thick and thin.

—Age 34

Do not keep the alabaster boxes of your love and tenderness sealed up until your friends are dead. Fill their lives with sweetness. Speak approving, cheering words while their ears can hear them and while their hearts can be thrilled by them.

—Henry Ward Beecher

A friend is a present you give to yourself.
—Robert Louis Stevenson

∾

*B*e mindful that happiness is not based on possessions, power, or prestige, but on relationships with people you love and respect.

$\mathcal{I}$'ve learned that ...

. . . if you're not willing to move mountains for your friends, they won't be willing to move them for you. —Age 18

. . . one of the best things I can give a hurting friend is my presence, not my words.

—Age 38

By friendship you mean the greatest love, the greatest usefulness, the most noble sufferings, the severest truth, the heartiest counsel, and the greatest union of minds of which brave men and women are capable.

—Jeremy Taylor

$\mathcal{R}$ekindle an old friendship.

❧

$\mathcal{O}$ffer to leave the tip when a friend invites you out to eat.

❧

$\mathcal{C}$all before dropping in on a friend.

Life has no blessing like a prudent friend.

—Euripides

❧

It is one of the blessings of old friends that you can afford to be stupid with them.

—Ralph Waldo Emerson

*L*ook for opportunities to make people feel important.

❧

*W*hen friends offer to help, let them.

❧

*W*hen you hear a kind word spoken about a friend, tell him so.

$\mathcal{I}$'ve learned that . . .

. . . the best remedy for a bad day is two cups of hot chocolate with marsh-mallows, a plate of chocolate-chip cookies warm from the oven, and a friend. —Age 31

. . . there are good neighbors wherever you live. —Age 30

$\mathcal{T}$wo persons cannot long be
friends if they cannot forgive
each other's little failings.

—— Jean de la Bruyère

∞

*$\mathcal{A}$ faithful friend is the
medicine of life.*

—Ecclesiastes 6:6

A friend is a person with whom I may be sincere. Before him I may think aloud.

—Ralph Waldo Emerson

☙

Ask someone you'd like to know better to list five people he would most like to meet. It will tell you a lot about him.

$\mathcal{B}$e open and accessible. The next person you meet could become your best friend.

∞

There is nothing so great that I fear to do it for my friend; nothing so small that I will disdain to do it for him.

—Sir Philip Sidney

$\mathcal{I}$ 've learned that ...

. . . when you're too busy for your friends, you're too busy. —Age 48

. . . no matter how good a friend someone is, they're going to hurt you every once in a while and you must forgive them for that. —Age 18

A true friend is the gift of God.

—Robert South

❧

Friendship has the skill and observation of the best physician, the diligence and vigilance of the best nurse, and the patience and tenderness of the best mother.

—Edward Clarendon

With every friend I love who has been taken into the brown bosom of earth, a part of me has been buried there; but their contributions to my being of happiness, strength, and understanding remain to sustain me in an altered world.

—Helen Keller

*The only way to have a friend
is to be one.*

—Ralph Waldo Emerson

*R*emember that the shortest
way to get anywhere is to
have a friend traveling with
you.

$\mathcal{I}$'ve learned that ...

. . . it makes me happy to see the answering machine light flashing when I get home. —Age 18

. . . people love to get letters from friends no matter what the subject is or the length of the letters. —Age 22

Fortify yourself with a flock of friends! You can select them at random, write to one, dine with one, visit one, or take your problems to one. There is always at least one who will understand, inspire, and give you the lift you need at the time.

—George Matthew Adams

Two persons cannot long be friends if they cannot forgive each other's little failings.

—Jean de La Bruyère

❧

The loss of a friend is like that of a limb; time may heal the anguish of the wound, but the loss cannot be repaired.

—Robert Southey

$\mathcal{I}$ve learned that ...

. . . you shouldn't judge people too quickly. Sometimes they have a good reason for the way they act.

—Age 20

. . . people will remember you as being a great conversationalist if you mostly listen.

—Age 49

*R*emember that no
time is ever wasted
that makes two
people better
friends.

Love and friendship are the discoveries of ourselves in others, and our delight in the recognition.

—Alexander Smith

❧

Friendship is the only cement that will ever hold the world together.

—Woodrow Wilson

$\mathcal{M}$eet regularly with friends
who hold vastly different
views than you.

∽

$\mathcal{D}$on't forget that a couple of
words of praise or
encouragement can make
someone's day.

I've learned that ...

. . . the definition of a best friend is someone who listens to me and knows that I will always return the favor.

—Age 23

. . . it's not the big things that you do for your friends that they remember; it's the little things.

—Age 62

In poverty and other misfortunes of life, true friends are a sure refuge. The young, they keep out of mischief; to the old, they are a comfort and aid in their weakness; and to those in the prime of life, they incite to noble deeds.

—Aristotle

$\mathcal{I}$'ve learned that . . .

. . . whatever your life lacks, such as parents, sisters, or brothers, God will give you a substitute and it usually takes the form of a wonderful friend. —Age 39

. . . it's never too late to show your friends you appreciate them. —Age 23

$\mathcal{W}$hen a friend is in need,
help him without his having
to ask.

∽

$\mathcal{C}$all three friends on
Thanksgiving and tell them
how thankful you are for
their friendship.

Go oft to the house of thy friend, for weeds choke the unused path.

—Ralph Waldo Emerson

❧

When a friend gets a new car, tell him how terrific it looks and ask to go for a ride.

$\mathcal{I}$'ve learned that . . .

. . . when I want advice, I call my best friend. When I want sympathy, I call my boyfriend. —Age 48

. . . no matter how serious your life requires you to be, everyone needs a friend to act goofy with. —Age 21

When someone you know is down and out, anonymously mail him or her a twenty-dollar bill.

❧

Send a "thinking of you" card to a friend who's experiencing the anniversary of the loss of a loved one.

*W*hen someone hugs you, let them be the first to let go.

True friendship is like sound health, the value of it is seldom known until it be lost.

—Charles Caleb Colton

When you see someone sitting alone on a bench, make it a point to speak to them.

∾

*Think where man's glory
most begins and ends,
And say my glory was I had
such friends.*

—W. B. Yeats

A friend may well be reckoned the masterpiece of Nature.

—Ralph Waldo Emerson